A Small Sneak Peek at

I f*cking Love You

AN IRREVERENT ADULT COLORING BOOK

BY SASHA O'HARA

ALSO BY SASHA O'HARA:

Calm the F*ck Down

Chill the F*ck Out

Cheer the F*ck Up

Happy f*cking Holidays

Calm the F*ck Down
Coloring Calendar & Planner

Cheaper than Therapy
Coloring Journal

Peace, Love & F*cking Happiness

Badass Chronicles
A Journal for Snarky People

Acknowledgments

I loved creating this book. It's been one of my favorites (though I love them all).
I hope it brings you as much laughter, fun and stress relief as it's brought me.
I'd like to thank my better half, for giving me so much inspiration for this book, and laughing at the sayings along with me (I know I can be a handful!) Thanks for loving me enough to be in on the joke. I f*cking love you, and will keep loving you until I forget who you are.

To Autumn, as always. You are my snarky doppleganger who helps keep this sassy Sasha gal going.

To Caroline King, for the I love you more than a Unicorn fart illustration. I mean, it's awesome, right?! Reach Caroline at: shironinjadeviantart.com and shiro-ninjatumblr. com

To Erica T., you're always so sweet to me, I really appreciate it. Thank you for the "You're MY asshole" quote. You must have some crazy love going on!

And to all of my fans, thanks for being you. Thanks for playing with me, for supporting me, for being sweet to me, and for sharing the snarky love. Smooches!

Last but not least, to the geniuses who came up with these kick ass sayings, because they are hilarious and true. Thank you.

Note

If you know me then you know that I have a *bit* of a snarky, smart ass, irreverent sense of humor. These pages are meant for fun and humor. Underneath that is a deep appreciation for real love and mutual respect in all relationships.

This book is for entertainment only, and no harm, actual or implied, is meant on any of these pages.

CONTAINS ADULT LANGUAGE
NOT INTENDED FOR CHILDREN

COLOR TEST PAGE

Let's make fun of people together

sugar is sweet.

LEMONS ARE TART.

I love you more than a unicorn fart.

You had me at "We'll make it look like an accident."

You can't make someone love you.
You can only stalk them and
hope for the best.

I love you so much. Except when you snore, zzzz then I want to PUNCH you in the face.

if you love
someone
let them go.
if they come
back no one else
wanted them.

I love you more than coffee

(but please don't make me prove it)

You
can stay but
your clothes
must go

Love means
not having
to hold
your farts
in anymore.

You're going to love the Valentine's Day plans you told me to make.

I love you,
but please die.

Sometimes I wish you were more fluent in silence.

I didn't say it was your fault

I said I was blaming you

My love for you burns stronger than my UTI

©Sasha O'Hara, www.sashaohara.com

I'm sorry we fought.
I hate it when you're wrong.

Sorry for judging you, your friends, your family and all your major life decisions.

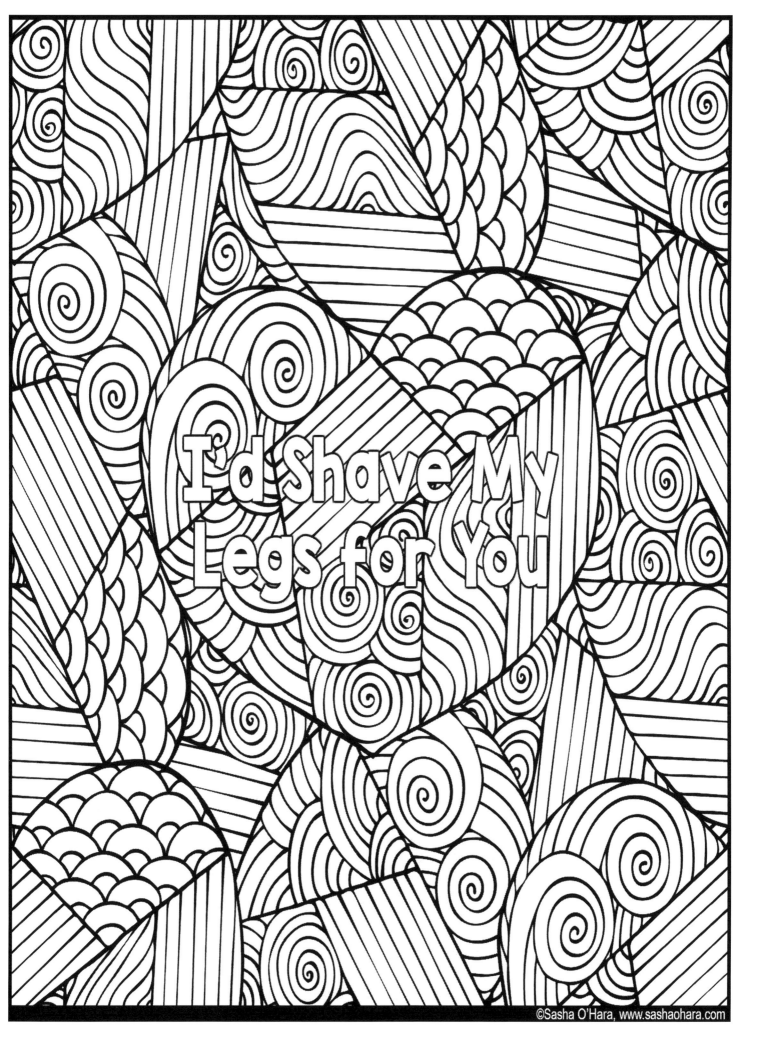

I am not needy. I am wanty.

I love you more than I did yesterday.
Yesterday you really pissed me off.

Thanks for purchasing this book.
I hope you're loving the sh*t out of it!

As a thank you I'd like to offer you
FREE DOWNLOADABLE BONUS PAGES!

Bonus pages include 5 more love illustrations not
included in this book, plus hand-selected love-themed
pages from my previous coloring books.*

To Download Your Bonus Pages Go to:

WWW.SASHAOHARA.COM/ifckinglovecoloring

*When you download your bonus you'll also be subscribed to
the Sasha O'Hara Society Newsletter. You can unsubscribe at any time.

Once again, thanks for purchasing this book
and for being a fan.

Happy coloring!

xoxo,
Sasha O'Hara

The only thing worse than Valentine's Day without you is Valentine's Day

You are an asshole. But you're my asshole.

May your new relationship last longer than that seal on Shark Week

I'm having a hard time getting over the relationship we were never in

Well aren't you just a little
lollipop triple dipped in psycho

I'm so committed to this relationship I've already let myself go

As long as you keep loving me I can keep hiding my crazy.

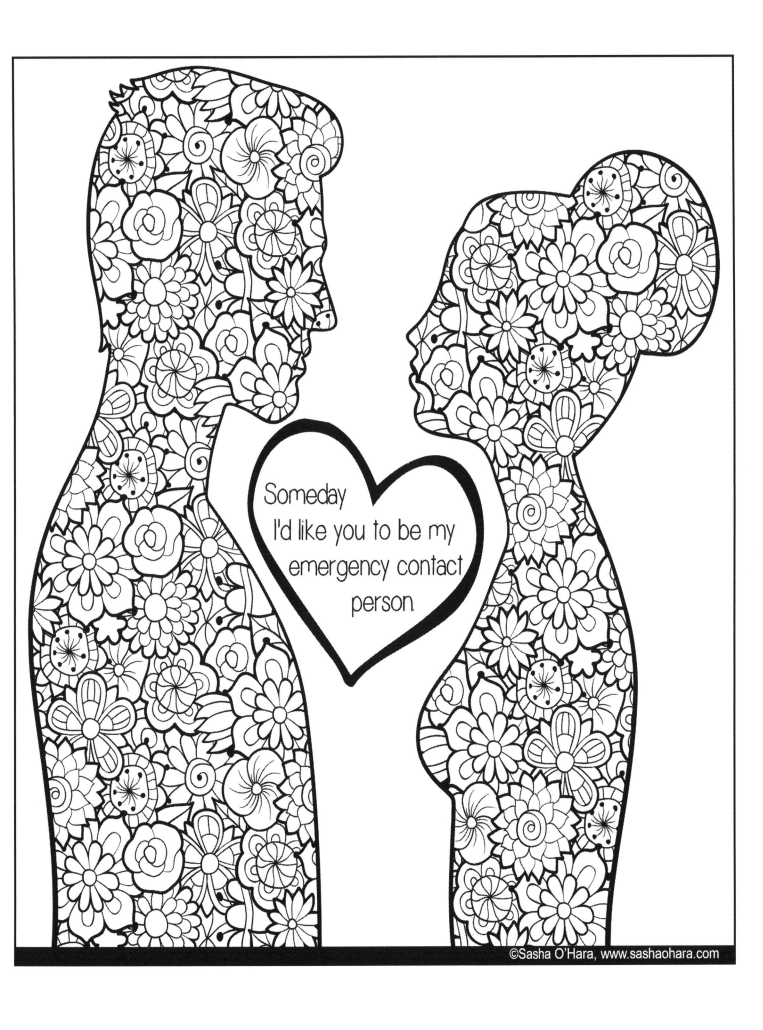

Someday
I'd like you to be my
emergency contact
person.

I think we need some time away from each other forever.

You annoy me more than I ever thought possible.
But I want to spend every irritating minute with you.

My ex had a very annoying habit.

Breathing.

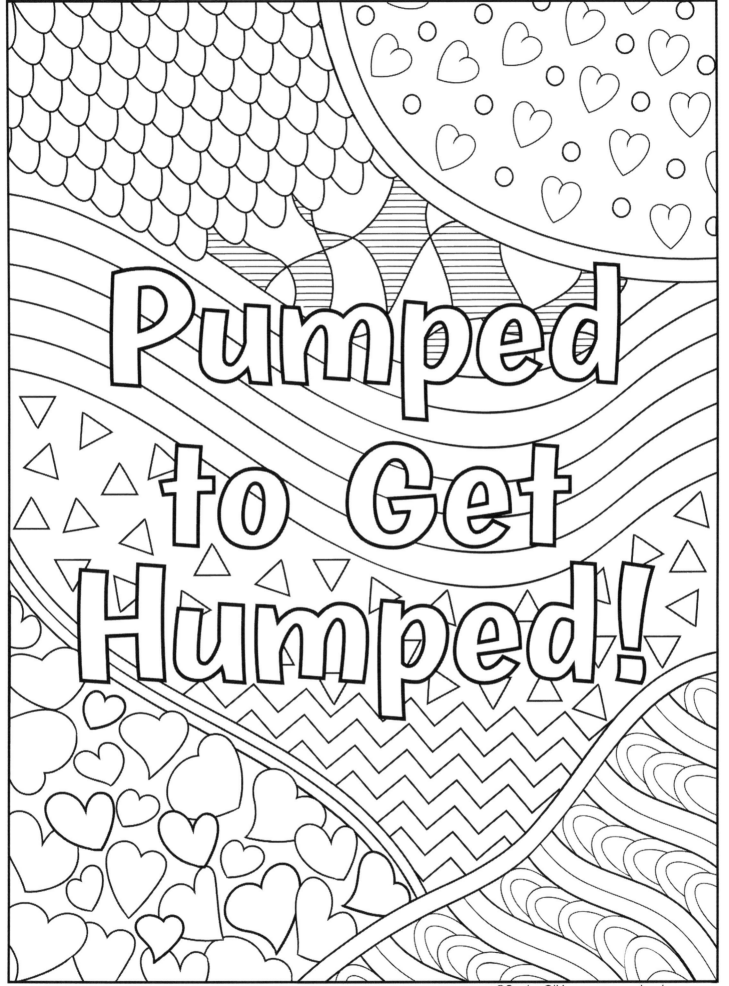

Of all the people I love, you're one of them.

a special gift for for you.

you're welcome.

I love you enough
to pretend I love you all the time.

admit it

life would be so
boring without me

Just thought you should know my ex got me really great Valentine's gifts.

You put the fun in dysfunctional.

It's not me. It's you.

I don't need to flirt. I will Woo you with my awkwardness

If you're reading this it means I let you live.

Thanks again for purchasing this book!

I hope you f*cking love it.

Let's Keep In Touch!

You can find me online at:

www.sashaohara.com

Where you can get that kickass newsletter I mentioned

And On
Facebook, YouTube and Twitter

All of my books are available in downloadable eBook format at:

www.sashaohara.com/shop

Made in the USA
Las Vegas, NV
11 February 2021